# PROVISIONAL CONCLUSIONS

# PROVISIONAL CONCLUSIONS

Poems about ADHD, Grief, and
Some of Life's Other Little Struggles

MIKE FEDEL

**iUniverse**

# PROVISIONAL CONCLUSIONS
## Poems about ADHD, Grief, and Some of Life's Other Little Struggles

iUniverse books may be ordered through booksellers or by contacting:

iUniverse
1663 Liberty Drive
Bloomington, IN 47403
www.iuniverse.com
1-800-Authors (1-800-288-4677)

ISBN: 978-1-4917-7994-1 (sc)
ISBN: 978-1-4917-7993-4 (e)

Library of Congress Control Number: 2015918478

Print information available on the last page.

iUniverse rev. date: 02/12/2016

# Provisional Conclusions

"These are fresh, moving poems by Mike Fedel, an important new voice in music and now in poetry."

**Anna Boothe**
author, *I Already Love You*, *Beyond Words*, and *Buddha*

"I was most powerfully moved by 'Back to the House', 'No More', 'Amy and Her Dad Do the Laundry', and the October 8th poem that starts with 'Lisa asked me what was wrong...' I was either very moved or devastated by them. ADD'ers just seem younger than their age. When you get to be our age, it's generally a good thing. We're not stuffy old men. Lots of men, in our culture at least, seem to get very rigid as they grow older, both in their thinking and their emotions, and ADD guys seem to do it less."

**Larry Letich, LCSW-C**
Counseling and Psychotherapy Services
author, *Where I Come From* and *This is a Man*

# The ADHD Chapter

"The ADHD section of Mike Fedel's poetry is peppered with the screaming realities of the 'inability to execute tasks.' He portrays a relationship with his own speeding brain. His self telling is direct and honest, as in:

> *Put all of my "to do's" behind a wall and take them out one*
> *or two at a time and actually finish them.*

"But such strategies only work for a while--the only consistency is inconsistency. So his emphasis turns to capturing the ideas flooding his ADHD brain, as in *Tomatoes*: collecting and archiving the failed opportunities, 'and not planting anything', frozen in overload.

"Lastly, he visits the self judgment that weaves its sinister imbalance throughout the sea of his life experience. Confessing 'I'm Sorry I Broke Your Life", pursuing his quest to find solid ground, and loving those that understand and forgive him.

"This is the poetry of a brilliant, often misunderstood ADHD mind, trapped in a linear world.

"His heart is loud and clear.

**Suzanne Ostrowski–Dansel, M.Ed., ACC**
Licensed Teacher
ADHD Coach

# Loss

"These are powerful and poignant poems which capture a father's experience of losing his 8 year-old daughter in an auto accident caused by a drunk driver. It is a searing account of how such a traumatic loss changes you forever, ripping yourself from the person you once were. He catalogues the emptiness of a lost future, where 'There are Holes so deep, Even darkness cannot reach the bottom.'

"Fedel insightfully recognizes how physical pain may be sought as a distraction from the intolerable psychic pain of losing one's child and coping with the brutality of an unfair world. Yet despite the loss that knows no end, in the beautiful 'A Sister Sunset' there is also the intimation of making a spiritual, lasting connection with one's lost child through an immersion with other similarly bereaved souls and the daily beauty of the world.

"Those who have had such a loss may find these poems very helpful by voicing the inarticulate depth of their grief. For those who have been spared such a trauma, it will help them to better understand what that loss feels like."

**Irving Leon, Ph.D.**
Licensed Clinical Psychologist
Adjunct Associate Professor of Obstetrics and Gynecology
University of Michigan Medical School and Health System
Author, *When a Baby Dies / Psychotherapy for Pregnancy and Newborn Loss* (Yale University Press, 1990)

*To everyone else*

*who's lost a child to a drunk driver*

*or*

*a life to an undiagnosed condition.*

*Provisional Conclusions*

# CONTENTS

## PART I
### Thinking Out Loud

## PART II
### The ADHD Chapter

## PART III
### Loss

## PART IV
### Love and Nervous Energy

# ACKNOWLEDGEMENTS

I owe my deepest thanks to the following people, without whom this collection would still be a stack of papers buried in my basement.

My friend Catherine Powers, both the poet and the woman. From the days of writing for the "underground" newspaper at Sacred Heart to sharing stories about broken water heaters and frozen pipes, your intelligence, honesty, and sense of humor have both challenged me and encouraged me to go deeper, be more open, and remember that these are poems, not lectures. You are amazing and I'm glad God, Fate, and our parents put us in the same neighborhood. Here's to the future of our shared sandbox (annarborpoetsonline.blogspot.com).

My high school English teacher Mary Jo (Oleszyk) Crane. You were the first person who took my writing seriously, certainly long before I did. Even when it careened from rock music to teen-aged lust to God, you always managed to make a comment that brought out some new dimension I hadn't considered. I'm also grateful for how much you did to get our work out to the public. From readings at the Henry Ford to workshops at Cranbrook to "Auguries" (I still have both issues), you helped us take ourselves seriously as writers, not just as students doing homework. Thanks.

Tom Cayley, my lifelong friend and partner-in-crime, who's always been there in the front row cheering me on and has a lot more confidence in me than I do.

My friend Joanne Henry, performer, educator, theologian, and jazz singer. Your conversations keep me in touch with the real world in a way few others can. I am blessed to know someone who lives at the intersection of so many of the things that matter to me. And thanks for introducing me to Bruce Cockburn's music way back when.

Larry Letich, whose poem "This Is A Man" reclaimed space for all of us at ADDA 2013 in Detroit. Having you say "not bad" about my ADHD poems would have been good enough for me. The fact that you actually liked them is humbling and makes me keep working to do better.

Jordan Meiller, writer, musician and friend, for comments, conversation, and convincing me that yes, I do need to read these out loud.

My friend and fellow performer, Nicholas Mourning. You and Mr. Electric Ocean gave me a new way to think about writing. The love and respect with which you handle your subjects - both in your writing and in your performing - is continuously inspiring to me.

Friends and family who helped me pick and choose: my mom, Michelle Slaviero, Nichole Hamilton, Connie Fedel, Karen Bamsey, and Sarah Lewis (who we lost in 2011). Only credit them with the ones you like. The rest were my choice.

My friends on North Maple in Ann Arbor.

And last, but not least, my family: to Amy for giving me eight years of wonder, enthusiasm, and love; to Lisa (whose poetry was in print well before mine - you go, girl!) for road trips, t-shirts, wizard rock and Five Year Mission, and for sometimes letting me pick the music; and to Jean, steady partner of 35 years, for toughing out the pre-diagnosis years (also known as the "who IS this guy?" years), for always being there, and for not serving me that chicken dish you made at your apartment back in 1974.

# PART I

# THINKING OUT LOUD

# MAYBE THAT WAS RICHARD BRAUTIGAN

I looked over the edge of the canoe.

There was a trout swimming
alongside just underneath
a leaf that was floating
on the surface like a candy bar wrapper
dropped by a small boy named Joey
who was walking
with his father
to a birthday party.

They were a few minutes late.

# PROUD DAD
*- for Lisa, her first year away at college*

Pride
is when she calls home and says
she spent the night
in her friend's dorm room
taking care of her,

not because she was drunk,
or had a headache,
or had a broken leg,

but because she was homesick.

# LOVE LETTERS

It never occurred to me that
if I carved your initials
and my initials
into a desktop at school
it might define me
forever.

That your initials
would follow me forever,
would always be somewhere nearby.

Maybe in the shadows.
Maybe in the back of my mind.
Maybe reading my Facebook page.

Maybe as a subtle vibration resonating at
exactly the same wavelength as
my fondest wishes and
wildest desires.

It doesn't matter.

I never had a knife when I needed one.

# TOURIST
# OR
# A REFLECTION
# 50 YEARS
# AFTER EXITING
# THE BIRTH CANAL

I want a better map.

Actually, I'd be happy
with any map at all.
I lost mine
when I got here.

Maybe I dropped it.

# SKETCHED IN PROFILE:
# THE THIRD DIVISION OF PLATO'S LINE

Everything is profile,
outline,
sketch,
approximation.

Everything is indicated,
pointed-at,
referred-to.

The center never fully gels.

Nothing does, except
maybe a slice of pizza
left out overnight
because something else
more important
had to be done.

The fantasy of the concrete—
that we can grasp Truth
and have Knowledge
beyond context,
absolute,
understood once and for all—
is so precious and naive
it makes me smile.

It's the same sad kind of smile
I get when I see the pizza
on the counter the next morning.

# EARLY GENDER CONSCIOUSNESS

How typically female of her
to think that was typically male of me.

# DREAMS

a small flower blooms
high in the mountains of Tibet
at the wrong time of year
in an environment in which
it cannot survive

a small flower blooms
in the crack between two bricks
too late in fall
in the street where they parked the car
after the shooting

a small flower blooms
between dreams and nightmares
just before i wake up

when i open my eyes

it's gone.

# LATE ONE NIGHT IN CLEVELAND

It's a little after
three in the morning.

I've been wheeling you
through the quiet halls
of the hospital,
where a sacred silence
fills
room after room
where other parents
sit
wait
hold vigil
hold their breath
anxious about tomorrow's surgery
or the outcome of yesterday's.

It's the first time you've been awake
since the team—
we never actually called them "the team"—
opened a small boney window
in your head
that let them remove 4 cm
of scarred temporal lobe
and ten years of
hallucinations
panic
ruined play dates
missed birthday parties
isolation

and a future
uncertain
but certainly not lived
without constant supervision.

You spot the chapel
and ask me
to take you inside.

There's a
stained glass window
there.

Light is shining through,
lighting it up
from the inside.

Light is shining through,
lighting you up
from the inside.

You look at the window
and start talking.

I sit down
at the piano
and start playing.

Loud enough
that I won't overhear
Your Conversation
Your Thank You
Your Celebration
Your Prayer.

But, soft enough
that I can still hear
Your Laughter.

*Provisional Conclusions*

# SCIENTIFIC PROOF OF E-MINOR

We were arguing about whether
or not Love could be reduced
to something scientific,
to a set of chemical reactions
in the brain.

Her argument was that,
since we could induce those feelings chemically,
we had proven a purely biological basis for them.

"Love" is only the name we give
to that particular brain activity.

I didn't make my usual
chicken-and-egg
argument. It hadn't worked before
and it probably wouldn't work now.

Instead, I asked her
"does the e-minor chord exist?"

She said "of course,
you just flat the 3rd."

I told her that the
e-minor chord did not exist.

There is only this: the action
of hammers hitting strings
causes the strings to vibrate.

This vibration creates sound waves
which travel through space
and cause a series of events
that travel
from eardrum to ear bone
to thousands of tiny hair
cells inside your inner ear
which your brain then interprets
as a sound.

"e-minor" is only
the name we give
to that particular brain activity.

She went home to think about that.

Our next argument
is scheduled for Saturday at around 2.

# THE MEN IN MY FAMILY AREN'T TALKERS

Fingers drumming on the table,
that's what I remember best about Grandpa.
That and his garden.
And walking with him on Dix Avenue.

His garden was bigger than our backyard,
bigger than our house,
bigger than our entire neighborhood.
At least that's how I remember it.

His fingers drummed, drummed, drummed
while he waited for his cheese
sandwich and coffee.
His coffee was more than half milk.
He was already drinking lattes in the 60s.
We just didn't know it.

I miss him.

He talked sometimes about the Old Country,
sometimes.
He had World War I and the Depression
inside his head.
His trip from Italy, the Nazis,
his mother and father,
his memories of my dad as a boy.

All inside his head.

The cheese sandwich usually had tomatoes
fresh, sliced tomatoes.
From his garden.

"What was it like being my dad's dad?"
I asked quietly.
Too quietly.

He drummed his fingers on the table.
Played solitaire.
Stirred his coffee.

*Grandma Anna and Grandpa Joseph Fedel*

*Phuket Buddha*

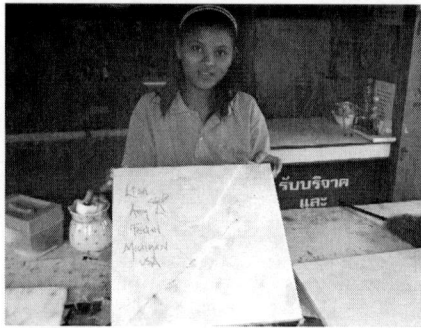

*Marble tile donated for Phuket Buddha*

# THE MISSING FISH

A long time ago,
I thought I saw something
in my bottom drawer
underneath my socks and underwear.

It didn't belong there.
It should have been in a fishbowl
or in the little pond
in the backyard
or on the second shelf in the basement
in the section where I keep my book
on bicycle repair.

The next time I saw it,
or thought I saw it,
was in a train station
in Unterschleißheim.

A Gymnasium boy
was showing me
how to use the box that stamps the time
on your railway ticket.
I bent down to pick it up
but my hand came up empty.

Damp,
but empty.

*Provisional Conclusions*

I thought I saw it
crossing the street
in front of my car
while I was at a red light
in downtown St. Paul
but I'm pretty sure
it was just a girl in a beige sweater
and navy blue shorts
whose shoulder bag
was too small.

*(I was lost once in the hills*
*in Phuket, Thailand.*
*I wanted to go see the big statue of the Buddha*
*on top of the hill.*
*I wasn't going there to pray.*
*I was just impressed by the size,*
*by the scale,*
*and by the idea that people would still*
*still*
*donate more than 30 million baht*
*to build a giant statue*
*of Gautama looking out over their bay.*
*There is now a square marble tile*
*somewhere in His robes*
*with my daughters' names on it*
*and a small drawing*
*of an angel.)*

I looked for it
in every box in the basement
and in the planter
that was here before we moved in,
although I was fairly certain
it wasn't in any of those.

Now,
all these years later,
I'm not even sure I really saw it in the first place.
Maybe it was just the reflection
of the early morning sun
off of an overused adjective
that was the exact color
of her hair.

# DURING A FRIENDLY GAME OF CARDS

There was a noise outside.

It wasn't much of a noise, just a loud "bang"[2]. I tried to ignore it but couldn't. I turned my head just in time to see the tall man enter the saloon. He was dusty, like he'd been blown across the fields of Oklahoma in May, 1934[1]. His skin was sunburned red leather, his hair thin, grey, and shoulder length. He'd never read Joyce or Emerson though once, on a long trip, he'd thumbed through a copy of "For Whom the Bell Tolls" looking for quotes for a speech he thought he might someday have to give.

Garrison barked for me to bring my attention back to the table. I looked at my cards. Eight of Hearts, King of Clubs and a picture of a unicorn standing beside a pen-and-ink drawing of a damsel in distress[3]. She looked so real I thought she might get up off of the card and walk across the table. She might push two more of my chips into the pile. The pile wasn't very big and I guessed most of them would fold if I raised.

Sam drew a pistol[4] and pointed it at me.

"You selling brushes, Lou?"

I shook my head.

"Never have, never will."

We'd played the game a hundred times but it never stopped scaring me. Sam wasn't too stable, even after all these years. Two of the players folded but Garrison kept playing. He raised me another two dollars.

I turned to Sam. I considered telling him that Garrison sold brushes on the side but thought the better of it. I never attended Catholic School[5], but I knew that God was watching us all the time. I was pretty sure God was the one who kept Karma working. It was the only way I could make sense of it all.

The tall man leaned against the bar and made a strange sound. A cloud of dust trickled from his mouth and floated across the room. It landed on the piano keys more than three weeks ago and I just now noticed it. The piano player wiped it off last Sunday, but now it was back.

He tried again, and this time he ordered whiskey. The bartender poured him a shot. He gulped it then said, "another."

"What about the damage to my front wall?"

"From the vase?"

"From the vase."

The man took off his hat and shook it. The dust fell straight to the floor in a neat pile[6]. He dropped his hat on the bar and reached for his gun-belt. He unclipped a medium-sized leather sack. He rested it on the bar and started to open it.

"I'm sorry about that. The Missuss. She sometimes gets a little frisky." He untied the string[7] at the top of the sack. "Now, friend, I have to tell you that I have no money in here, but I have a fine collection of brushes that you could bring home to your wife. Or maybe your girlfriend[8]?" he winked.

Sam turned his head.

I knew that the rest of the night would not go well.

-----------------

*Provisional Conclusions*

# NOTES

2. I didn't know until just now that the noise had been a ceramic vase smashing into the side of the building. His girlfriend, Daisy, had thrown it as him after he dismounted the horse and made it clear that he was going into the saloon to "look for some company." I didn't know because I couldn't have known as I hadn't written it yet.

1. "A gigantic cloud of dust, 1,500 miles long, 900 miles across and two miles high, buffeted and smothered almost one-third of the nation today," a United Press story in the Hastings Tribune of May 11, 1934 reported. He probably wasn't in that storm, but he could have been.

3. Alicia wasn't really a damsel-in-distress but she often did nude modeling for artists who worked in either charcoal or 2B and 3B pencils.

4. Sam's pistol was especially important to him in that it had been handed down from his grandfather to his father and then to him. Both of them had used it to shoot brush salesmen they'd suspected of seducing their wives.

5. I actually did attend Catholic school, but my character did not. They had no Catholic schools in the town in which my character grew up. I would tell you the name of the town, but I haven't decided yet. It will be somewhere in the Midwest, though, I'm fairly certain of that. Most of the towns my characters grow up in are in the Midwest. Most of them have a mean annual temperature of 98.6F.

6. The pile was actually in the outline of a square. Nobody believes it, so I decided not to tell you.

7. The string was actually a twenty-inch piece of catgut. On one of his trips 94 weeks and three days ago, he'd met a violin player who was changing his strings. They got to talking and the man offered him the catgut because his bag was untied. The tall man wasn't interested until the violin player explained that 'catgut' was not actually made from the guts of a cat, but from the intestines of various other

animals. In this case, a pig. The tall man was reassured that no cats had been injured just to bring Brahms to the West. He accepted the catgut and a small book of Persian poetry in exchange for the cord from an electric battery charger. He'd been using that to tie the bag closed but it never quite held.

8. It was -- and still is -- not uncommon for men to make jokes like this with each other. They are pathetic attempts to relive one's glory days -- when one might actually be able to maintain both a wife and a girlfriend. Everyone knows it's a lie and everyone goes along with it. We all laugh. It's like catching a large bass and throwing it back, very, very late at night.

# IN A LARGE STACK OF PAPERS
# TYPED ON AN OLD ROYAL QUIET DELUXE
# WHICH IS STILL IN MY BASEMENT
# – SOMEWHERE

There are four screenplays living in my head.

There were others but they left.

They complained before they left
that their living space was cramped and dirty
and that they didn't like the other screenplays
some of whom were bullies
and some of whom were just lost and confused
and at least one of whom smelled of Old Spice.

The ones who stayed will leave eventually
when they realize that I left the door open.

# ON A DIRT ROAD
# IN THE ORIENT
# A VERY LONG TIME AGO

He stood outside the tent for a long time before anyone came out.

The man who emerged was well dressed, though his clothes were now rumpled and his hair disheveled. He was sliding a gold bracelet back onto his wrist. He saw the other man standing outside and averted his eyes. Then, just as quickly, he turned his head again. Their eyes locked.

His eyes were defiant. Who did this man think he was? Judging him. Walking around the countryside talking about his "great insights" and "new vision" of how things were and how they should be. He knew the type. Nietzsche would write about them nearly two thousand years later. They were failures and they blamed the Others for their failure. The Ones who had the Will to take what They wanted from life. The Ones who didn't shrink from what Had To Be Done. The Ones who defined the Language, who made the Rules, who decided What Could and What Couldn't be done. Who was and who wasn't valuable.

The other man's eyes were different. He wasn't angry. He wasn't jealous or upset. He simply saw a man coming out of a tent. Everything else was construct. While he was growing up, he was taught to believe this and that. Then something came to him and now it was all different. He had been looking for something and now that he had it, it was his duty to share it. Nothing more, nothing less.

The flap of the tent opened again. The woman looked out and up at him. She smiled. He looked behind her and saw a red pillow.

*Provisional Conclusions*

# OAKLAND, 1993

Three little girls walking
down Piedmont Avenue,
holding hands
fairy princesses
*blackwhiteblack*
fast friends.
Everyone loves everyone.
It takes a village.

Later, on the bus,
a mother
*blackwhiteblack*
yells at her five year old who
is too excited about what he sees
out the window.
"Sit down! Shut up!"

My car is broken down
again.
I'm broke too.
The man
*blackwhiteblack*
who comes out of the alley to help
can't get it started either.

He gives me twenty dollars
for cab fare home.

In the grocery store,
a woman
*blackwhiteblack*
tells her daughter
not to talk to
mine.

Young men selling bean pies
outside the Safeway
won't even look at me.

# LA PETITE MORT

everyone fears death

it is
Ultimate Surrender

everything changes

subtle shifts
in ever widening circles
from the point of origin
out through every thread
in the fabric of time and space
ever
touched
by
you

everything changes
for you
for your Lover
for your Family
for your Friends
for the Universe

nothing is the same afterwards
and everything that went before
takes on new meaning

we fear death
but
maybe we want it
maybe we need it

maybe we need just a little bit of it

# ON DUTY

One thing that is always absolutely magical to me
is the sight of the first icicle of winter.

It's exciting.

Not quite Christmas morning exciting,
or new bike exciting,
or 'going camping at Waterloo
and yes Tom can come' exciting,
but close.

They hang from tree branches
and the wheel wells of cars
and overhead wires,
pointing at the snow
with such precision
you wonder if each icicle
has a particular snowflake
it has been assigned to keep damp.

# TUNE UP

Here's part of my List:

- get to bed on time
- eat better
- get more fresh air
- cultivate gratitude
- read more about ADHD

The List goes on
for two full pages.

When I checked under my hood,
I didn't expect to find
so many opportunities
to do things
that cost so little money
and so much time.

I seem to be
in that 98%
who want a
magic bullet, a
miracle cure, a
quick fix
that I can squeeze in
between tasks
and pay for
with the money I make
during all the time
I'm not spending
on me.

*Korean War Memorial, Washington D.C.*

*Dad*

# IN THE RAIN
*- for my dad, who served in Korea 1951-1954*

They stand in the rain,
motionless.

Nineteen of Them,
stainless steel,
each over seven feet tall
watching for
something.

They will watch forever.

We stand there,
in the rain,
three of us,
flesh and blood
and freedom.

It's cold.

We go back to the car,

because we can.

Duty done, airplanes and paperwork
brought Them back home.
At least one of Them
made his way back to Detroit
to do what he could
for the neighborhood kids,

making art with clay and IBM punch cards
and building a robot (shhh, don't tell anyone,
it's just a refrigerator box
painted silver).

Later, he would buy a coffin
to scare the trick-or-treaters
and an amplifier from Sears
so I could be heard
over our drummer.

He never talked about it,
my dad,
not that I remember.
Now, 54,246 bodies
and 60-some years later,
we hear noises and see shadows
and look around
wearily
for new answers
to very, very old questions.

The Average precipitation
in depth (mm per year)
was 1054
in 2009.

It's still raining.

# KORCZAK'S ROCK
(a visit to Crazy Horse Monument)

We drove move than sixty hours to get there.

Not all in one day, of course.
We stopped all along the way
to sleep
or to eat at Casey's
or Mama's
or wherever the locals ate.

There was no rush.
The mountains would be there.
They'd been there forever.

They were Sacred space.

They were Sacred space long before we decided to visit.
They were Sacred space long before the Six Grandfathers
became the four presidents.
They will be Sacred space
even after the monument was finished.

It was as inspiring as I'd read.

The project had been going on since 1948
(or 1929 if you ask Henry the Elder).
We had no idea about the plans
for the campus
for the medical training center,
no idea
of the breadth and depth of the vision.

I met a Woman there
in the visitor center.
She was making beaded jewelry.

We talked about where to buy beads
and about making art
and about selling crafts.

We did not talk about Religion
or Ancestors
or History.

I told Her I sometimes felt guilty
making my designs out of tiny beads
after seeing all of the
moccasins and pouches and necklaces
in the museum.

She gave me a look
and said,
"get over it, white boy."

A few hours before we got there,
I'd seen three Women
sitting at the roadside
near the cemetery at Wounded Knee.

I didn't ask Them any questions.

They didn't look like They wanted to talk.

They had a job to do
and that job was selling handmade dolls and scarfs.

I thought that at such a holy place,
it would be different.

Back in Custer County,
Thunderhead Mountain listened
to me
not talking.

Somewhere in the back of my mind
I wondered this:
if Crazy Horse was not still
buried deep inside that rock,
would he ride over
and ask me why I only talked
to the Woman who was indoors?

*Crazy Horse Memorial, Black Hills, South Dakota*

*Happy Man, beadwork by Mike*

# UNRAVELING

mosquito
snake
spider
bee

There is a long list
of things I don't understand
but I know that the web is fragile,

so I walk around them
instead of stepping on them.

I don't tug
at loose threads on sweaters either.

# PROMETHEUS AND ATLAS
# AT THE TYPEWRITER

The words of this poem
strain and groan,
doing their best to carry the full weight
of the conclusions I want you,
dear reader,
to draw.

Neo-colonialism,
forced assimilation,
and postmodern deconstruction of classical texts
have left us with nowhere to turn for direction
except traffic lights and advertising—
neither of which can be relied upon
in a real emergency.

Without a steady supply of electricity,
only poems like this
stand between us and
chaos.

Why can't you see that?

Of course, these are only my
provisional conclusions.
Nothing is static, nothing guaranteed.

Maybe I need bigger words.
Weightier ones
that have been peer-reviewed and cross-checked
in double-blind studies,
all variables defined
and controlled.
Absolutely controlled.

Or, maybe I should expect a little less
from 26 simple characters.

Think.

# HOWARD (WASHINGTON) THURMAN

In the office on Larkin Street
there is a bust of Dr. Thurman.

I would often sit alone at the desk
after the bulletins were printed
after the phones were answered
after the mail was sorted
and stare.

Nothing happened.

Nothing visible.

But everything inside me grew
until it overflowed
with love.

He walked down these same halls.
He preached from this same lectern.
He heard music from that same piano.

Did he ever sit in this chair?

A small number of people know about him.

He chatted music with Gandhi.
Listened to Tagore underneath a banyan tree.
Dr. King carried his book in his pocket.
Morehouse College has a dorm with his name on it.

He wrote poetry
and painted penguins.

He understood Centering Down
and Common Ground.
Maybe more than anything else.

Maybe more than anyone else.

I brought my daughters to his church.
I made music there.

The building is still there.
2041 Larkin Street,
San Francisco.

Go visit it.

# WHY A GARDEN?

Why a garden?

I wonder that sometimes.

It doesn't keep me up nights.

It doesn't grab me
like the question "why evil?"
or the question "why free will?"
or even the question "why craving?"

But it is curious.

A place of beauty
a place of rest
repose, tranquility
and whispered secrets
that keep two people going
for another ten years.

Kids run, still free
birds sing, dogs pee
elders sit on benches and feed pigeons.
Lovers laugh.

And somewhere,
twenty centuries earlier,
he nervously fingers a small bag of silver coins
and waits for the man he is going to kiss.

# HELL

Small, scratching sounds.
I laugh. They've tried that before.
The sound continues, so I keep laughing.
I hear it all around me but I don't feel it.
I reach for my face.
My mouth is closed.

The room is completely black.
Something scurries over my foot.
I feel the long tail.
This is cheap horror film crap.
I am not scared.
This is not hell.

Small, scratching sounds.
The light flickers.
Something leaps at me out of the corner.
I feel teeth tear into my knee, thigh.
I'm somewhere bad.
Not hell.

Small, scratching sounds.
My own finger,
scratching a scab on my leg.
I watch fascinated
as the blood starts to flow.
Have I gone insane already?

*Provisional Conclusions*

The light comes on.
My daughter is in the next room.
She presses her nose to the dirty glass
and looks through.
Figures stir in the shadows.
"Papa?"
One of them grabs her hair and pulls
her backward
into the darkness.

I feel something wet on my cheek.
I touch it with my right hand.
Blood.
The nails of my left hand
continue to claw at my scalp.

Small, scratching sounds
I scream.

I close my eyes.
I ball my fists.
Press them hard against my clenched eyelids.
I can still see.
I can still see what they are doing to my children.
Again.

Calloused, clawed feet walk across the floor.
Two of them stand in front of me.
Bright red skin.
Talons.
Black, black eyes.
Stench.
Sulfur.

"Are you real?"

# PART II

# THE ADHD CHAPTER

# WATCHING FOR CRACKS

He doesn't know
how many fish are in the lake,
but he doesn't need to know.

He knows not to try and catch them all right now.

It can't be done.

There would be no point anyway.
He knows he can only sell so many on a given day.

On Saturday,
he helped me put all of my "to-do's" behind a wall.

We sawed a small opening near the bottom
so I could take them out one or two at a time
and actually finish them.

It worked for a while, but
now I find myself staring at the wall
nervous,
anxious,

watching for cracks.

# TOMATOES

I imagine
that somewhere,
there is a man who keeps
track of his regrets.

He writes them
in spiral notebooks
and stores them
in his two-car garage
in boxes sealed with yellow tape.

I imagine the garage filling up,
and now, he has to add a second story.
And now, he has to build a shed next to the garage
to keep his gardening tools (and his saw).

He wanted to grow tomatoes. Reference:
(Box 8, notebook 26, p 4)
(Box 22, notebook 7, p 16 & 24)
(Box 22, notebook 8, p 4, 11, 73)
(Box 46, notebook 16, p 91)
(others)

Even though he says he wants to grow tomatoes,
the gardening tools are rusty and unused.

I imagine walking past his house one day
during planting season and seeing him
through the window,
sitting at the dining room table
with an open notebook in front of him
writing,
writing,
writing,

and not planting anything.

# I'M SORRY I BROKE YOUR LIFE

The books I read—
the ADD books—
talk about
blurting and
losing things and
being impulsive and
taking risks and
appearing not to listen.

What they don't talk about are
the nights I got up—
the nights I get up—
after everyone is asleep
and take out the glue and tape
and the box where I keep
all the jagged little pieces
of your life before me.

Of what you wanted to be and
what you might have been and
what you should have been
and
I try to put them back together.

I feel like a kid
who's locked himself in the basement
and is trying to fix the lamp he broke
before mom and dad get home.

The work always goes badly.

I'm not even sure that I have all the pieces.
I chipped them away slowly over the years.
I saved the ones I could find,
but I'm scared that I don't have them all.

And even the ones I have,

I really don't know what to do with.

*Provisional Conclusions*

# A SINNER VISITS PARADISE

all around me, I see people
trying to do the right thing

i am not one of them

i'm just trying to find solid ground
so i can have somewhere to sit down
and rest

i am trying to find my memories
so i can visit my daughters
in those early days
when we splashed in puddles
and danced in the rain
and didn't have to worry about
whether the green moss
on amy's headstone
could be scrubbed off

i am trying to find a way
to deal with the bad wiring
inside my head
that makes me tell lisa h
that of course she has time to volunteer
she's never had to hold down a real job
or makes my friend write
"dear mike, or is it God?"

i am trying to find a place
where i can either feel love
for a world that's trying to do better
or contempt for a world that's given up

augustine and st paul
both wrote about knowing what to do
and not being able to do it

welcome to our world, guys
we call it "inability to execute"

a long time ago,
sarah convinced me
that the kingdom of god
is already among us
really

she found it
she has a small cottage there

i visit it once in a while

before i go, i make sure i take my meds
i'm pretty sure i'd offend the people there too

# A SMALL GLASS BALL
(A FAIRY TALE)

Once upon a time,
a long time ago,
a little girl handed
a little boy
a small glass ball.

He didn't know what it was,
but he knew it was a gift.

He threw it in the air
and caught it a few times.
Then, he tried to bounce it on the floor.
Only it didn't bounce.

It cracked.

He got angry
and picked it up
and threw it again, harder.

It cracked a little more
and something leaked out.

What?
He couldn't tell.
He didn't recognize it.
Maybe it was a girl thing,
something the little girl's mother
had whispered to her a long time ago
when they were both still young.

The little girl smiled
and picked up the ball
and wiped it off and polished it
and handed it back to the boy again,
hopeful that,
this time,
things might be different.

★

Once upon a time,
a long time ago,
a little girl handed
a little boy
a small glass ball.

He didn't know what it was,
but he knew that it was a gift.

He wanted to give her a gift too.
He brought her many different things,
things he'd collected and kept.
His secret things.
But she didn't know what they were.
She didn't recognize the shapes
and, besides, they spun much too fast.

They slashed and shred mercilessly.
Her fingers bled,
even as she tried to say "thank you"
and make sense of them.

What were they?
Maybe frantic dreams?
Maybe frenzied ambitions?
Maybe all of the somethings
he thought were possible
when he was still young.

*Provisional Conclusions*

Still, the little girl smiled
and picked up the ball
and wiped it off and polished it
and handed it back to him again,
hopeful that,
this time,
things might be different.

# TRUING UP THE CORNERS
# OF A LIFE THAT IS MOVING
# VERY QUICKLY BUT
# ALONG THE WRONG TRACK

several things are out of kilter
here in this small room
where i write and draw
and make up songs
that i don't record
because
several things are out of kilter
here in this room
where i move piles of paper
from one end of the desk to the other
expecting that somehow
something will reveal itself
that will help me correct the fact that
several things are out of kilter
here in this space
that i've carved out between
teleconferences and bedtime stories
and "did you take out the trash?"
i don't know
why i can't balance all of this
how hard can it be?

*Provisional Conclusions*

# FRAGILE

Everything in front of me is fragile
and could easily break
into a million pieces.

The wall behind me is brick
it is solid.

The slab I'm laying on is granite
it's solid
it's cold
and that's O.K.
it's better than O.K.
it's solid.

I could get up and start my day
but everything out there is fragile
and is going to break
into a million pieces.

# PART III

# LOSS

# ARCHAEOLOGY:
# VISITING OUR HOME
# SIX WEEKS AFTER AMY'S FUNERAL

I went to the house today.
These are my notes:

It feels like doing archaeology.

I'm looking at all the things these people used—
the books on their shelves,
the toys in one of the rooms,
clothes in various closets.

Whoever these people were, they probably had two kids—
there's two small beds with
canopies in one of the bedrooms.
In the closet in that room, there
are kids clothes in two different
sizes.

Girls clothes.

English was evidently the primary
language in the home—
all the books are in English.
Over two hundred kids books in
the smaller bedroom.
Ranging from Dr. Seuss
to
Beverly Clearly
to
Judy Blume.

Full set of Shel Silverstein's books
and Peter Alsop's records.

Nothing very unusual about
the bathroom,
kitchen,
dining room.

Not much food in the refrigerator,
but I understand they've been away.

Maybe someone cleaned it out for them.

Signs of pets, but none around.

Piles of unanswered mail on
the dining room table.


I wonder who they were.

# PORTRAIT OF A GHOST

I wanted to paint her.

I wanted to make
a portrait of a ghost.

I wanted to capture the
emptiness
and the sense of calm
even in uncertainty.

I was anxious.

All I had to work with
was a box of brittle pastels
and some clay modeling tools my dad left me.

The portrait came out badly.

The composition was flawed.

Not enough to ruin the picture,
but it was obvious something was missing.

I think what was missing
was the melody.

There was no sense
of sound and motion.

She was stiff and formal
no matter how much I tried
to convince her to relax.

# EBERWHITE PLAYGROUND,
# SEPTEMBER 15, 1998 - 1:18 A.M.

Last night, just after midnight, I found myself
wandering in the playground
at Eberwhite Elementary School.

I learned some things.

I learned that it's pointless to stand there
in the dark calling your kid's name
when you know she's been killed.

She won't answer.

She won't come.

She won't put down the ball,
tell her buddies goodbye,
and run over to your car.

She won't grumble
and ask for "just five more minutes."

She won't complain that it isn't fair that she has to
stop playing with her friends just to go pick up her
pesky little sister.

She won't ask you to walk back into the school building
with her to get her backpack or let her make a quick
trip to the toilet.

She won't jump up and throw her arms around your neck,
wrap her legs around you and yell "daddy!"

She won't say "I know you're going to say no, but can
I go play at Fumika's house when we get home?"

She won't jump into the front seat and say "Papa, guess
what we did today!" or "Papa, guess what Julia (or Marie
or Calyn) told me today!" or even "Papa, what does it mean
when you 'give someone the finger'?"

None of this will happen.

You'll just stand there
feeling a little too cold,
with the light from the building shining
just a little too bright.

You'll feel stupid and
over-dramatic and self-indulgent
for standing there
with tears and snot
dripping down your face
calling the name
of a child
who
you
know
is
dead.

*Amy's Roadside Cross, I-75 near Indian River, MI*

# 2 WEEKS OR 30 YEARS LATER: GRIEF GROUP

It was our job
to protect them.

Now,
we say things like this:

*Her father:*
I should have
told her not to see him anymore
or
told her to break up with him
or
told her that he was dangerous

or

*His mother:*
I should have
known something was wrong
when he came home too early
or
when he was being too quiet
or
when he was sleeping too late

or

*Me:*
I should have
taken a different road
or
left earlier or later
or
not gone at all.


There are Holes so deep
Even darkness cannot reach the bottom.

# PAIN AND MEMORIES

Wear shoes that are too tight.
Then walk around a lot.
Stand near things that make loud noises.
Stare wide-eyed into the sun.
Press an ice cube into a sensitive tooth.
Make another paper cut on your thumb.
Bang your shin against the desk.
Slam your head into the door jamb.

Pour salt on your tongue.
Pour lemon juice on your tongue.
Pour Tabasco on your tongue.
Pour scalding hot tea on your tongue.

Get back into the body,
out of memories,
out of hope,
out of fear
and longing.

Wear shoes that are too tight.

# ALL MEN ARE CREATED EQUAL

Dad's got his five year old boy with him
in the hotel room next door.

They are watching Monday Night Football.
I hear dad's yelling through the wall
"Fuck him up bad!"

I close my eyes
and breathe
and remind myself
what I've been taught:
Love thy neighbor.
All men are created equal.

------

In the therapist's waiting room,
a ten year old boy runs in crying to mom
"dad hit me, can I stay in here with you?"

Mom takes a drag off her cigarette
and answers, "I don't care what you do,
if you want to stay, stay."

Wonder what the kid's thinking.

I close my eyes
and breathe
and remind myself
what I've been taught:
Love thy neighbor.
All men are created equal.

Sometimes, I wonder.

------

Dad's got a fifth kid on the way
but it's Friday night
and "no bitch is keeping me home."

A few shots and a pitcher later
bar's closing and it's time to leave.

He doesn't see the red light,
runs the intersection,
kills the six year old.

I close my eyes
and breathe
and remind myself
what I've been taught:
Love thy neighbor.
All men are created equal.

Sometimes, I think "do I really have to believe this?"

------

Dad's working two jobs
money's tight,
car's barely holding together.

Exhausted, he
coaches his daughter's soccer game.

Frustrated, he
scrapes together ten dollars for her field trip.

Scared, he
takes her to the doctor to look at the tiny spot on her arm.

I close my eyes
and breathe
and remind myself
what I've been taught:
Love thy neighbor.
All men are created equal.

Sometimes. Sometimes.

# AMY AND HER DAD DO THE LAUNDRY

1.

In the guest's laundry at our hotel
there's a folding table.
On the table is my laptop.
Behind my laptop, there are two spigots
recessed into the beige plasterboard wall.

Near them to the left,
the electrical outlet
I'm using to power this laptop.
Near them to the right,
some phone numbers
scribbled in pencil.

These spigots have blue handles
hexagon handles like the kind
in the backyard.

Wondering what they are for,
I turn my head
and see that there are three more.
Those three in use,
one for each of the washing machines.

I think:
If this fourth one was in use
I wouldn't have a table to write on.

Thank you for small favors.

There's some lint
in the bottom of the recessed box they're in.
They are dusty from disuse.

They don't remind me of Amy.

2.

This laptop has a 386 processor and a grayscale monitor
and a customized version of Nibbles.

Nibbles was one of the games distributed with early
releases of DOS—runs under QBASIC.

I hacked the game for her, added more interesting mazes
and hardcoded a slower speed for the little cursor that
runs through them.

She carried this clothes basket
up and down the stairs for me.

Most of the clothes in it are clothes she's seen me in.

It's raining, starting to turn cold.
I don't remember if she was scared of lightning storms.

What else will I forget?

3.

Halloween just passed.

Last year, she was a bride.
This year she probably would have been a Spice Girl.

Mom and Dad would not let her dress like
Olivia Newton John in Grease
and she didn't know
what the girl from the Titanic
looked like.

Last Halloween,
I brought her little sister to school.
They paraded through the halls together.

Some other kids brought younger sibs too.
It's that kind of school.

Just a few weeks before she was killed,
Amy was explaining to her little sister
that, during assemblies,
Lisa would get to sit on the floor
at the front of the auditorium
because she was in kindergarten

Lisa was excited about that.

At day care, the kindergartners were the oldest
and had to sit in the back.

4.

What happened:

We finished dinner at Big Boys
She read in the back seat with the light on
Finished her book
Put it down and said goodnight
Was killed

5.

*(Drunk and Happy in America - 1)*

A guy digs into the pocket of a
worn out, favorite pair of jeans.

He finds his keys, fumbles.

They crash to the ground.

Picks them up and laughs out loud.
No one's around—who are you laughing for?
He laughs again—louder
he yells his laugh to the sky.

After a few passes, the key finds the lock.
He turns it and the button pops up.
He pulls the door open and climbs into the cab.

Fingers of his left hand circle the ignition.
The index finger of his right hand feels for the slot.
He tries to push the key where his finger was.
Laughs when it fails.

"Can't find the hole, eh?"

He turns his head.
Outside, a friend's just pulled up
and thrown his joke through the open window.

Driver laughs at it.
Puts his head on the steering wheel.
Tries to regain his composure.

Hard to see.
Tears are streaming down his cheek.

That was pretty damn funny, get it?
Can't find the hole?
hahahaha
Such a funny joke calls for a drink.

His friend's already inside.

He gets out of the truck.
Manages to get the keys back into his pocket.
Walks back into the bar.

6.

Some level of success

I got the clothes from the washer to the dryer
without thinking about the times she and I played
in the basement
me throwing the damp clothes to her a piece at a time
so she could "help me with the laundry" and so I
could spend some time with her doing things I knew
she would probably grow to hate

7.

I listen to an angry mother who talks about a child molester
who got probation.

Email from a student whose brother was stabbed 22 times by
the jealous ex-lover of a homeless woman he'd taken in.

Someone in a chat room complains
about being sold the wrong color vehicle.

I listen to Bruce's song about children missing legs
after stepping on landmines in Mozambique.

The size of the tragedy grows and shrinks
depending on the light I shine on it.

Maybe that's normal.

How big is the tragedy of a dead child?

And why should I give a shit about anyone else's pain?

8.

A long time ago.

San Francisco
a BART station, probably Powell Street.
A man in his 40s or 50s dressed in dirty clothes
leans against the wall
takes a few stumbling steps
bumps into someone.

Amy asks what's wrong with that man
is he sick?
We're aware of the line—
illness or
moral judgement—
we tell her it's an illness.

For years, the story and the question are with us.

When we see beer ads
when she sees people passed out on the sidewalks
or in parks
in Oakland
in Berkeley
in San Francisco.

She talks this out with mom and dad.

The agreement in our house is:
no more than 2 drinks on a given night
no more than 1 night a week.
If we are out, one of us has a glass of wine.
The other one drives.

She's concerned.
Why do people do this to themselves?
Can't President Clinton just close down all the bars?

I don't want to try and explain to her
about liquor lobbies
and the Free Market
and the amoral nature of commerce.

At the same time
we want her to learn about the line between 'freedom' and 'license'
we want to let her know that actions have consequences
we want her to know that addictions exist
we want her to know about making good choices

So we tell her what we can.

It's gratifying and mysterious to me
that she's concerned about these people and
what they are doing to themselves.

She isn't yet fully aware
that actions have consequences.

Someone else decides to teach her that lesson himself.

9.

The dryer continues to rattle on behind me.

I'm not impatient like I was
when it was her T-shirt for soccer
and the game was in 20 minutes

or

when it was clothes for a weekend trip
and the longer we waited for them to dry
the later we'd arrive to check in
and set up camp

or

when it was the top she just had to have
to wear to school on picture day.

I guess that's a good thing.
Patience is a virtue.

She's been dead for three months
and we are slowly recovering.

Lisa is still not Lisa,
Jean is still not Jean,
I am still not me
and Amy is still dead.

Time will change some of these things.

10.

*(Drunk and Happy in America - 2)*

The woman is angry,
spilled red wine on her white dress
"it will never wash out!"

Someone suggests soda water
and hands her a glass.

She takes it gladly and stands up
pushes back her chair
nearly falls,
catches her balance.

Weaves her way through the crowded restaurant
bumping into tables,
men who leer,
women who push back,
one tray that topples.
It is a very, very long walk.

In the ladies room she splashes the stain
pats it dry
splashes again
pats it dry
holds it under the hand dryer.

"White wine for me"
she laughs when she gets back to her table.
That will avoid any further damage
to her clothes.

The others have already eaten dessert
coffee still to come
and Sambucca to complement the dinner.

Then, a twenty minute drive home.

*Provisional Conclusions*

11.

Little sister Lisa
is back in the hotel room, asleep.
Survived the same car crash.
Lives with TBI and seizures.

I think about yesterday at school.

I was embarrassed by her mouse.
It was just a big black blob of paint.

She painted broadly
covered the legs
head
tail.

I wanted to protect her.
I asked her to draw it again.
I kept telling myself
"this is the wrong thing to say"
but I couldn't stop myself.

I want to see her run again.
Instead, I watch her limp toward the classroom.
Her weight is on her instep—
the bones in her left ankle look deformed,
her 45 pounds focus on that one joint.
I imagine bone ripping through flesh.

I watch a videotape of her
April 1998
her birthday party at Leslie Science Center
running
digging
opening her presents
thrilled
helping her friends find a dinosaur bone on the "dig."

I want *her* back too.

12.

The dryer stops.

I hear the wind whipping through the
not-quite-tight door jamb.

I want to sit here
until that eerie sound
becomes Amy's voice
and her ghost
comes to visit me.

*Lisa visits Amy on her birthday, 2001*

# A SISTER SUNSET

He was sitting at one of the little round steel mesh tables
outside the coffee shop. I stopped a few feet away and
sipped my coffee, watching him out of the corner of my eye.
He was watching the sunset.

The sunset is one of the few things
I can get completely lost in.

It held his attention completely.
No new dad watching his baby girl sleeping
or hunter waiting for a deer to come closer
(closer, just a little bit closer)
could have been more intently focused.

I recognized the look
because that is exactly the same way
I watch sunsets.
I get lost in sunsets.

Once, I rode a motor scooter up Chao Fa Road to see
the giant Phuket Buddha. At one point, the road became
more and more narrow, then it was a footpath, then it was
gone. I was alone. I did not speak the language
and none of my friends knew where I was.

A sunset is that kind of lost.

I stood there for nearly half an hour watching with him.

I left first.

[NOTE: a "sister sunset" is our family's name for a sunset that reminds us
of Amy. Her last words were "a sunset is nature's way of saying goodnight."]

# MY UNCLE MIKE

My Uncle John played guitar.

So did my Uncle Mikey.
And tamburitza
with the Detroit Tamburitza Orchestra.

I have a cassette tape of Uncle Mike
playing at a festival in Las Vegas
and another cassette tape of a broadcast
of the Detroit Croation Radio Network.

At one point,
the announcer thanks Elizabeth and Michael Pojen
for their financial support toward building
the National Shrine of the Little Flower
in Royal Oak, just north of Detroit.

The Tower there was built in 1931.
It was built of stone.
The Ku Klux Klan burned a cross there in 1926
when the church first opened.
This was a cross they could not burn.

Mikey left behind a box full of tapes
of him and his brother making music,
and a prim
with only 4 strings.

Some nights, I tune it up and play along,
thinking of backyard pig roasts in 1962
and my first sips of Budweiser.

# PART IV

# LOVE AND NERVOUS ENERGY

# WHY WE DO THIS

When a ball's dropped,
it falls. It is trying
to minimize its gravitational potential.

Planets orbit around the sun
along the exact path that allows
them to maintain an equilibrium between
the centrifugal force of their travel
and the gravitational pull of the sun.

We do this, too.

We will continue to do this
forever
because we're reached a steady state
between the way you stir your coffee
and the way I change my guitar strings.

# HAPPY BIRTHDAY TO LISA
*- for the Bronies*

Did I really
use "birthday"
as today's writing prompt
just so I could
say
"happy birthday"
to my daughter?

.

.

.

.

.

.

.

.

.

*ee-yup*

# BEDTIME
*- for Lisa and Amy*

At nine o'clock, we'd go upstairs
Well, more or less at nine
Bedtime was kind of flexible
(you learned that watching mine).

So, sometime after sundown, you'd
wash up and brush your teeth.
Upstairs, I'd check the bed, again -
nope, nothing underneath.

We'd settle in for story time
you holding Rupert Bear.
I'd do my best to make one up
while you finished your prayers.

We had our favorites, you and me,
if there was nothing new
inside me on a given night,
the old ones worked for you.

Another "Walking in the Woods"
with music at the end
(or) a new "Page Of The Story"
featuring all your friends.

The characters were not the same
on any given night—
some reappeared from time to time
I guess that was all right.

*Provisional Conclusions*

You'd lean your head there on my chest,
I'd kiss and stroke your hair.
I'd feel you warm, I'd feel you safe
in those moments we'd share

a universe of love. I'd stay long
after story's end
I wish that I could lay with you
and feel that way again.

# IT'S A BEAR, PAPA

"This little brown circle
with the lines coming out of it
is a bear."

You told me that.
i remember the moment.

i'd looked over and
must have smiled at You.

i didn't know that You knew
i didn't know what it was.

Your face beamed.

You were so proud of that bear.

# DIRTY DISHES

*"All your talk is worthless*
*when compared to one whisper*
*of the Beloved."*

Rumi said that "I Love You" is love of God,
no matter who is sitting across the table from you
when you say it.

I am comfortable with that.

The idea that what I love
is God–in–you
is easier than thinking
that I love you–as–you, especially
when the trash is overflowing
and the sink is full of dirty dishes.

# BRIDGEPORT

My dad had his own key.

Anytime he wanted to,
he could just drive there
and go in
and do finish work on
beautiful brass pulleys.

Piecework.

(He and I made a lot of money that summer.)

He had his own key.

He could unlock that green metal door,
click on the lights,
turn on the power,
and he and I could make pulleys
anytime he wanted to.

He showed me how to set up the lathe.
How to inch the carbaloy cutter forward slowly.
Just enough.
Just enough.

You have to shave the metal.
Shave it, not cut it.

*Provisional Conclusions*

He had his own key.

We could work for an hour
or we could work all night long
if we wanted to.

I would have worked all night long
but I had school in the morning.

# ON CAMPBELL STREET
# IN DEARBORN HEIGHTS, MI
# A LONG TIME AGO
# WHEN THE WORLD WAS STILL
# FULL OF POSSIBILITIES

She sat down.
The bench was about ten yards
from where I was sitting.

I know that
because later—
after she left,
after the birds were gone
and the paper bag had blown away—
I walked from here to there
and measured it.

She opened
the paper bag
without raising her head.

I watched
as she took out the bits
that would become the last lunch
I would ever see her eat.

She ate
a cup of yogurt
some sliced apples
a piece of cheese
a piece of chocolate.

She drank
a bottle of water
and something out of
a small blue plastic bottle.

She thought this:
*i wonder if i thought about it long enough*
*and worked at it hard enough,*
*i would be able to find that one moment,*
*that one single mistake i made,*
*that one thing that set my life on this path*
*and i wonder if i could go back and fix that?*
*if everything would change*
*if i would become the person i wanted to be*
*instead of the person i am?*

*i remember one night,*
*i was staying overnight at gramma's*
*and i wished on a star.*

*i wonder if i wished for the wrong thing.*

# A POETRY SEMINAR
# IN MICHIGAN
# IN 1974

Cindy—
no, Cynthia—
is waiting for Steve
to say something
about her poem
"California."

She looks
like an innocent woman
waiting for a verdict.

# ONE LATE AFTERNOON IN A COFFEE SHOP

It was just the slightest touch.

I think Van Morrison was playing.
I don't usually close my eyes in public
but the chair was comfortable
and I was sleepy.

Maybe not even a touch, maybe just her walking past me.

It was one of his mystical tunes.
Today was an exception.
Usually, I sat at a table
but, today, I'd committed to a day off.

There was a single green flower on sheer white fabric.

Van's music made me receptive.
Swimming in time and space,
my body had no boundaries.
It was Everywhere.
It was Everything.

Just the slightest touch.

Crazy Love.
One touch brought it all back.
All of my body's history.

I stood up.

# MY BRUCE COCKBURN FLOOR PLAN

"Fascist Architecture"
whispered to me that is would be
a song of scathing commentary
on the forces of political repression
or the silent fascism
of a regime that
equates shopping
with freedom.

But something was wrong.
He was singing the mirror
but it was facing the wrong direction.

I recognized the buildings.
I'd built them myself.
The ramparts and the towers were mine.
I built them.
I patrol them,
marching back and forth
in the dark,
defending them against foes,
imagined
and
imagined.

I've sung a lot
of his songs
to different audiences,
to my friends,
to my girls at bedtime.

I won't sing this one
until I can.

# ON GOING BACK

ain't never goin' back

# HAPPINESS
## (LESSON 1 - CAUSE AND EFFECT)
*- for Cy Udall, Loren Greenawalt, and David Vaughn*

Hume rolled over
and nudged Kant.
"Hey, bucko!
Wake up outta that dogmatic slumber!"

Hume lectured him for a while
about billiard balls and habit
and cause-and-effect,
then went back to sleep.

I don't exactly remember what he said.

It was early Sunday morning
and I was thinking about the fact
that most of the really happy people I know
are church musicians.

# ABOUT THE AUTHOR

Mike Fedel is a performer, writer, and educator who lives in Ann Arbor, MI. He holds degrees in philosophy, theology, and Performance Studies and recently went on "permanent sabbatical."

*Amy and Lisa, first day of school*

*Provisional Conclusions*

Edwards Brothers Malloy
Thorofare, NJ  USA
March 14, 2016